Thierry Rollet

Two sacred monsters

Boris Karloff and Bela Lugosi

Editions Dedicaces

TWO SACRED MONSTERS

Published by:
    Editions Dedicaces LLC
    12759 NE Whitaker Way, Suite D833
    Portland, Oregon, 97230
    www.dedicaces.us

Library of Congress Cataloging-in-Publication Data
    Rollet, Thierry.
    Two sacred monsters / by Thierry Rollet.
    p. cm.
    ISBN-13: 978-1-77076-526-9 (alk. paper)
    ISBN-10: 1-77076-526-3 (alk. paper)

Thierry Rollet

Two sacred monsters

Boris Karloff and Bela Lugosi

PROLOGUE

What artists were sought between the years 20 and 30?

The crazy years knew the argument that opposed the triumphant historical theatre to the stammering cinema, already risen to the rank of 7th Art. All campaigns in the West saw the quarrels between the ambulant theater groups and manifestations of a beginning "cinematography", which already sought to establish itself as a gender, if not dominant, at least called to take advantage of its presence to provide a future. So it is evident that such an argument, which is reminiscent of the Ancients and Moderns in European literature, had at the same time its opposing forces, but also its advocates – these latter being, of course, the actors themselves.

Actually, being an actor couldn't defend themselves, but by subjecting to all types of representation, being carried out on the scene or on screens. All actors of this generation made it a point of honor to give it their all for these two pillars of their talent, since they appeared to be one more promising than the other.

Well advised were also the actors who knew not only how to profit from the two genders, but most of all, alternate, passing from one to the other to assert and maintain their reputation.

Boris Karloff and Bela Lugosi were naturally from both categories.

True professionals, they had noticed that the new cinema presented an unmistakable resemblance to the theatre: that of "give to see", from the Greek work "theatre". Just like its millenary alter ego, the debuting cinema gave actors something to see, while maintaining the advantage of moving them more economically: finished were the exhausting tours and most of all, expensive! The cinema only carries its films, and not a group that has to be transported, fed and costumed. This new support, so promising, constituted an extra platform for actors, but not less.

In exchange, and since they were "given to see", the cinema of this decade, that often remained mute, asked actors for a body language and facial expression that the theater considered only as accompanying the text. No dialogue in the cinema, so all was in the expressions, in the most general sense of the word. Such an actor, not knowing how to stand, walk and most of all translate by the help of all the elements of his face the interpreted character, had no future in cinema. Therefore, alternating between theater and film in their work of interpretation made sense in the daily life of an actor. One could even say that a beginner learned to use his gestures and his face in the cinema to better support the text on the scene. Alternating the two genders proved to be a good learning experience.

Then, the cinema had sound and therefore, it imitated theater while retaining the economic benefits it had over it. Well-formed actors, well-trained, then felt even more at ease, without doubt. It's what determined their career, favoring the appearance of the two that later on would be called "sacred monsters".

With Boris Karloff and Bela Lugosi, this modern name would immediately take a double meaning.

CHAPTER 1

Two destines, similar and contrasting at the same time

What is being said about Boris Karloff and Bela Lugosi? What names come immediately to mind when these two actors are mentioned, so similar and so different at the same time? The answer: Frankenstein and Dracula. Moreover, the first is often mistaken with its creature, the second with its creator: Frankenstein is the monster, Dracula the vampire, while each of them is the result, for the first one, of the ego of a romanticized bio-geneticist, for the second, of a noble Magyar, equally legendary for his cruelty, who very early assimilated to a mythical being who existed before it[1].

Still, as far as our two actors are concerned, this common point was the real founder of their career and, *ipso facto*, the main anchor of their own legend with movie fans of all countries.

Curiosity, then, demands to know how they got there.

***

William Henry Pratt, alias Boris Karloff (1887-1969) and Bela Ferenc Dezső Blaskó, alias Bela Lugosi (1882-1956) knew from an early age what would make their future, namely attraction, magic, if not the madness of the scene.

William Henry Pratt would represent during his whole life what the Americans call the *self-made man*, the one who made it on his own. Indeed, in many ways, he is the incarnation of this American myth, while Bela Blaskó would rather be the one of the "classical" immigrant, which is to say, with a more or less ordinary destiny, having run from his country for economic and political

---

[1] See chapter 4.

reasons – while William Henry Pratt had left his only to get on immediately with what seemed to him a podium.

Without doubt, he felt this need, like a very natural given. William Henry Pratt, born in Dulwich, in suburban London, was the last child from a family of nine children and, having lost his parents at the age of three, he owed his education to a sister and his seven older brothers. By his own confession, he lived a childhood and an adolescence as pampered as was possible, but totally oblivious to the family tradition who would have wanted to see him become an official in the consular administration, where his father had had a career. Young William admired one of his brothers, George, who had known a brief stay in theatre: he then felt encouraged to imitate him, equally served by an innate taste for disguise and representation. So it was a more natural destiny that pushed him to interpret, as a child, the role of the "demon king" in a school adaptation of *Cinderella*.

A young man, William Henry Pratt quickly decided he wasn't made for studying, to which his older brothers wanted to confine him to, out of respect for the paternal will. His tastes, more and more bohemian, carried him more towards the theatre than the course rooms, as exams didn't represent any outcome in his eyes. At the time – a still young 20th century –immigration was encouraged, especially for those the society then considered as failures from birth. Therefore, he played toss with his future destination – Australia or Canada, promised lands to the "failures" and it was Canada that won. The year 1909 saw the young British land in Ontario, and then go until the west coast, in Vancouver, without a penny in his pocket!

So, no American dream – in the continental sense of the word – and especially, of success, like the colonist William Henry Pratt, who immediately realized that he wasn't made for agriculture, as he wasn't made for studies. Then, what would he choose? What was required: the theatre, always the theatre!

Yes, now, drawing now our attention to Bela Blaskó, we'll first discover that in the destiny of this other last child of a less numerous family – only four children – a copy almost the same to the beginning of life for the young British actor. He was also the son of an official of what was then the Austrian-Hungarian Empire, Bela Blaskó was born in Lugos, a city that passed, after the First World War, under the Romanian authority, but remained

10

nonetheless in the legendary Transylvania: the future "count Dracula" of the cinema saw the day in the country of vampires! Without doubt, it was a sign... even more evident than the one that maybe determined the future vocation of Boris Karloff for the role of the demon monster: it's in the theatre that he met his first fantastic character, when the future Bela Lugosi had it "in his blood", in some way, considering his birth place in a land of demons!

Just like the young Pratt, the young Blaskó was the despair of his family as far as studies and a professional career were concerned: embracing the civil servant career would have meant for both of them to give to life the kiss of Judas! Their common taste for the theatre represented their vocation, unshakeable as must any vocation worthy of the name be.

Still, Bela Blaskó had to wait to be 20 to start on the scene: Hungarian in an authoritarian country dominated by the Austrians, he couldn't hope to become an actor in his first youth and most of all, without any intellectual preparation, even if his self-willingness to learn is worthy of praise in such a context: he read extensively, exercising his memory on all kinds of texts to prepare for what he considered to already be his job. This tenacity paid off: on the recommendation of his brother in law, he began in a small traveling theater where he accepted all the roles he was offered. Thus, he became good enough to be noticed and join the National Theatre of Budapest, where, again, he played many very different roles, even that of Christ. This success was the reward of a long patience: Bela Blaskó, now known under the pseudonym of Bela Lugosi – for gratitude to his home city – was already 31 years old...!

Thereafter, if Henry William Pratt, because of his emigration to America, was spared from the first global conflict that was about to burst, it was not the same for Bela Lugosi who saw the war abruptly interrupt his career as an actor. Who knows what would have happened if the two young interpreters had met on the front, one a British, the other a Hungarian, soldiers in opposing armies? The military experience was reserved to the infantryman

---

[2] « I fished Karloff from Russian ancestors on my mother's side and for Boris I was inspired by the cold Canadian climate. » (Boris Karloff).

who could not go back on stage until 1917, having miraculously survived a serious injury – while William Henry Pratt, who had just chosen his stage name[2] was going between Vancouver (Canada) and Seattle (USA), accepting all the work he could find.

The Boris Karloff from then was considered like a very clumsy beginner: stage directors pulled their hair out seeing him entangled in the sets and experienced many difficulties replying to his colleagues during rehearsals which dragged on because of him. But they still kept him in the small group of Ray Brandon, who had hired him, for they had recognized that there was no one like him to interpret the roles of the "bad guy"; without doubt, it was due to his deep voice, to his solid bearing, served by a tall and powerful built, not to mention the extreme mobility of his features that fit all disguises – quality that foreshadowed his starring role, so far still…!

While Boris Karloff struggled on the scene, Bela Lugosi was already entering the seventh art born of the old Austro-Hungarian Empire. He first made a quiet entrance under a new nickname Arizstic Olt, and then turned it to Lugosi. Would he become a star of the screen? No doubt he would have had if events not prevented him, at least in his country. It is precisely there that a significant divergence appears in the two careers of Boris Karloff and Bela Lugosi. One knew the fate of a Cornelian hero seeing outside elements oppose his trade: the global epidemic of the Spanish flu in 1918 that temporarily closed theaters and a cyclone that destroyed the space where the theatre was located near Vancouver. Meanwhile, the other became a Racinian character rushing into the avatar that would be the cause of his own misfortune: politics.

Indeed, the old Austro-Hungarian Empire, conquered and dismembered after 1918, saw Hungary accessing into a Republican independence who was to deliver it from the Austrian oppression for good and assure it, in principle, a release to which, naturally all actors and artists aspired, eager for the freedom of expression. So it was with enthusiasm that Bela Lugosi joined the Liberal government of Karolyi, then the Communist regime of Bela Kuhn that overthrew him in 1919. Although more authoritarian than Karolyi's, the Kuhn Government approved the creation of the Union of Actors to which Bela Lugosi took to after creating it. However, Hungary hadn't finished with violence, including that of Bela Kuhn whose government ended in a terrible repression.

12

Romania was moved and favored a new revolution, which knew how to bring to power another dictator: Admiral Horthy, sadly famous, since he had to stay in power until 1944, thus becoming one of the leading European supporter of Nazism.

The two, Kuhn and Lugosi, were thus constrained to run from their countries, in danger of being arrested and imprisoned by the Horthy Police. They each took a different direction: Russia for the communist Kuhn, Austria for actor Lugosi, a country that had become a republic, being more welcoming towards artists. This tumultuous exile, nevertheless had adverse effects on the private life of Bela Lugosi: the actress Ilona Szmick, which he had married in 1917, asked for a divorce rather than following him to Austria.

Without money, without means of existence, Bela Lugosi then went to Berlin and played in silent films, rather than on the scene, for he didn't fluently speak German. Destiny showed itself then, since he interpreted a role in *Der Januskopf*, a German adaptation after *Doctor Jekyll and Mister Hyde*, made by one of the pioneers of fantasy cinema: Friedrich Murnau, of which I will have the chance to speak about later on[3]. Then, it was without doubt America that called him since he played the role of Chingachgook in a version of *The last of the Mohicans*, created by Arthur Wellin. Still, it was soon after, in 1921, that he succumbed to the American dream which was that of many emigrants, and above all, good actors. So, Bela Lugosi joined the land of Uncle Sam by a more direct way than the one followed by Boris Karloff.

The latter, during this time, had known an exhausting career that he was learning on the job, performing key roles this time in successful plays, but for which there was little pay. Leaving himself to the American dream, he wanted to leave Canada for Chicago, but the theatre was in the slump due to the war. Boris Karloff wanted to enlist, probably out of spite in the British army, but was discharged for "heart condition". Until 1920, he accumulated insignificant roles, but which ended up hiring him for a big tour towards western USA. A very difficult time for the young actor who supported himself by mixing his acting activities with delivery driver jobs. Nevertheless, it is what indicates his

---

[3] See below, chapter 3.

ability to be a self-made man in the US style, already emphasized in the beginning of this chapter.

Tenacity and unwavering commitment to serve the actor profession, as was then the common feeling, that by divergent paths animated the two actors during their difficult beginning – and even somewhat disappointing... !

***

It's in the early 20s that our two actors began to frequent the Hollywood studios. Indeed, the cinema growth, even the silent one, made the theatrical gender become obsolete. We remember that Bela Lugosi had already experienced in his country and in Germany a few acting experiences as a film actor. Boris Karloff was at the beginning, since he had until then only played the role as an extra, paid with 5 dollars a day in Douglas Faribanks' movie, *His Majesty Douglas*. Still, it was what determined the final orientation of his acting career since he too began to frequent the studio rather than theaters in order to find work – while continuing to earn his daily pay with small jobs. He had completely established himself in the United States by marrying an American dancer, Helen Vivian Soule – from which he will divorce in 1928.

It was in 1930 that Boris Karloff finally caught the attention of producers: having played the main role in Martin Flavin's play *The criminal code*, he was approached to take the same role when the Columbia company purchased the rights of this play. Boris Karloff, remarried with Dorothy Stines, then had notable meetings and got most roles thanks to his remarkable ability to disguise himself. He was well liked by the famous makeup artist Lon Chaney, and it was precisely this meeting that would really launch his career, as we will see later on.

During this time, Bela Lugosi knew the same difficult career, equally disappointing as his private life: two new marriages, the second one lasting only a few days, made him realize that the theatre career and private life were really irreconcilable for him. Nonetheless, unlike Boris Karloff, he never completely abandoned theatre, despite the tough competition of the cinema, who had become spoken. Accumulating small roles without importance, he was learning English, but in the way of a school boy, for he recited his texts better than he played them; indeed, he had never left the
14

Hungarian environment, since it was in a Hungarian community of emigrants that he owed his integration to and even his livelihood when he had first arrived in the United States. New York was then a mandatory stop for all European emigrants, a kind of back life that led them to the ghettos that still exist today. Still, it was this life that made the glorious life of Bela Lugosi.

Having interpreted at first roles of "bad guy" or foreign agent in low-budget thrillers for which his Hungarian accent destined him for, Bela Lugosi saw himself one beautiful day, in 1927, receive the role that would bring him fame: that of count Dracula.

Dracula was first a play, created in 1923 in London by Hamilton Deane, then bought in 1927 by the *Fulton Theatre* in New York. Naturally, they thought about Bela Lugosi to interpret the leading role: even if he was already 45, he had kept a young face, extremely mobile and apt to keep that cold and cynical expression that had to be, at the same time, the one of a demon and a seducer, as the role demanded. If we add the Transylvanian accent which characterized Bela Lugosi throughout his career, his commitment to this role became evident. The play had 261 representations and had a huge success to such a point that the cinema bought it and gave its realization to Tod Browning.

During this time, Boris Karloff's career also knew its first great start. Maker James Whale was thinking about adapting the best-seller *Frankenstein* by Mary Shelley. It was Lon Chaney, charged with makeup that introduced to him to the young aspiring actor that Boris Karloff had become. Still, other actors had already been approached to play the star role: that of the monster, of course! And one of them had been precisely Bela Lugosi! The latter couldn't accept, for he had just finished *Dracula* and he was already engaged in another leading role in the *Double murders in rue Morgue*.

This is how the cinema had approached these two actors, so stubborn and so tested, allowing their destinies to meet, like a sort of sign from providence, that serves the artists so well at times.

CHAPTER 2

Where the roads meet

Here are two favorite actors of fantasy cinema intersect and soon meet.

Moreover, most critics consider that the rising fame of Boris Karloff and Bela Lugosi owes much to what we now call "the golden age of fantastic cinema", that in turn, owes its reputation to the 7th Art in general: far from being a simple trend, as predicted – or hoped? – by the most ardent fans of theatre, silent and then spoken cinema, became a true social phenomenon that never disappeared, since, in our days, we can even see it in a very private way in the form of VOD (video on demand) on a smartphone. In those times, theatre rooms emptied at the benefit of theaters where the black movie superseded the melodrama of the scenes. Nothing surprising, in these conditions that this cultural tsunami should serve as a springboard – a feeble word! – for the career of our two actors.

Star of a day, star forever: this is what happened to Bela Lugosi as soon as he performed the role of Count Dracula. I have said it: it was especially this quasi-hypnotic gaze, well highlighted by a pale lighting and rendered cruel and terrifying by its ice fixity, which made the celebrity of the Hungarian actor – when Tod Browning was no doubt counting on the foreign accent of Lugosi to ensure a convincing interpretation of the Transylvanian vampire. In reality, Lugosi could combine luck with talent since Lon Chaney, both makeup artist and actor, was approached first to interpret Dracula. Destiny chose otherwise since Lon Chaney died in 1930 and the movie was launched the next year. It's not inconceivable to think, that it was Tod Browning who used his influence to ultimately hire Bela Lugosi.

Often enough, cinema contributed to the making of a star, putting it in the same roles or in the same type of movie: Armando Catalano alias Guy Williams only made the 80 episodes of Zorro at Walt Disney: Douglas Fairbanks shined in the gener of cape and sword; Gary Cooper won the prize of the adventure epics… It's like this that Bela Lugosi became, overnight, star of the scary movies, and this during the seventeen years after Tod Browning's Dracula.

It was at that moment that Bela Lugosi was approached to play the role of Frankenstein's monster in the adaptation made by James Whale. I said it in the previous chapter that he was hired for the interpretation of doctor Mirakle in *Double murder on rue Morgue*. Still, the rumors of the studios claim that Bela Lugosi had refused the role of the monster, when the famous makeup artists Jack Pierce had made him try the mask. At that time, an actor under contract couldn't allow himself to refuse a role, especially when he was becoming known: harder then, most definitive too, would have been his downfall! Rumors even specify that Lugosi would have declined this role because it was silent! It is true, however, that the director approached to shoot the film was not then James Whale, but Robert Florey. The dismissal of the latter turned the tables. The latter then offered the role to Boris Karloff, allowing him, in his turn, to shine like a real American star by the most powerful projectors!

Of this career crossroads, the two actors weren't really aware at that time, as they didn't personally know each other – nothing in any case, allows us to assert it. It had to the express will of Universal to meddle for Boris Karloff and Bela Lugosi to meet, to play together in the *Black Cat* in 1934.

At that time, Boris Karloff had himself wished to make a turn in his career, unless it wasn't as an aside. Becoming a star, he couldn't find a place in this tainted world, fleeing the social functions of this environment for the benefit of family life: married and father of a little girl, he kept – contrary to Bela Lugosi, it seems – the concern to continue his private life without it being invaded by social events. Furthermore, his new star status seemed to go hand in hand with an increase in his style, which he couldn't get from Universal. So he left Hollywood for British Gaumont in London – meaning a return to the sources! – who offered him a role in *The living phantom*. Unfortunately, the public didn't follow, and Boris Karloff saw himself taken again by America: he had made *The Mummy* two years before – still with James Whale – and had even attracted the praise of the critics and an immense popularity. *The living phantom*, which tells the story of an Egyptologist emerging from beyond to claim a stolen stone, was perceived like a feeble copy of *The Mummy*, better able to serve the main actor than to ensure its fame.

Boris Karloff returned to the United States and went to knock at the door of Hollywood again, where Universal studios, having themselves understood the lesson, offered him a more advantageous contract, where he benefited – a great favor – of the freedom to make other movies if he so desired: in every lord there is honor, you are or you are not a star!

It was then the idea came to make Karloff and Lugosi play in the same movie. I repeat, the two stars only knew each other by reputation and had never met, since Boris Karloff, contrary to Bela Lugosi, ran from social functions where actors and producers showed themselves in the same places! Of this first encounter was born the real shock of *The Black Cat*, somewhat inspired by the story of Edgar Poe[4].

I say "a little" because the movie script takes many liberties concerning the count's intrigue. Here, it's not about a spouse sinking into alcoholism and murdering his wife and hiding her in a wall, without realizing that his favorite animal, a black cat, is walling to betray him, and then by its desperate meowing. Carl Lemmle's *The Black Cat*, is the story of a fight between Verdegast (Bela Lugosi) and Poelzig (Boris Karloff): the first accuses the second, chief of a satanic sect, of having made his wife and daughter disappear. A young couple met by Verdegast in the train is strangely mixed in this intrigue: strangely, as we wonder, all along this film that would pass today as a short film – it only lasts 65 minutes – what exactly is this couple's usefulness, if this is to confuse the clash between the two stars without affecting their actors' play, always indicative of their ability to play cynical and animated characters, of a cruelty or a determination that are unfailing. As far as the black cat is concerned, it appears only fortuitously, in a single scene: one clearly wants to impress upon the viewer that it is the embodiment of the satanic spirit that reigns in this house, throughout this enclosure which is supposed to take place in Hungary – but yes! – although we don't notice anything typical in the rare outside scenes.

The wisdom of the director and scriptwriter was to give equal importance in the plot to Boris Karloff and Bela Lugosi. This was

---

[4] Published in New extraordinary stories, translated by Charles Baudelaire.

also the case in *The Raven*, shot the following year. Again, the two characters clash, although one, the criminal Bateman (Boris Karloff) seeks firstly the help of Dr. Vollin (Bela Lugosi) for a plastic surgery operation. However, the plot is complicated by the intervention of the Thatcher family, Dr. Vollin wanting to marry the daughter. Unlike *The Black Cat*, the character Bateman plays spoilsport, instead of the young couple in the previous film. The imprint of Edgar Allan Poe is always mentioned in the scenario, in a more obvious way yet, because it is doctor Vollin who is inspired, having built a torture chamber in his cellar for dominant instrument, the murderer pendulum presented in the tale *The Pit and the Pendulum*. The end turns the criminal Bateman into a positive hero, since he redeems himself by delivering Thatcher, thus preventing him from being slaughtered by the terrible pendulum. The moral will be saved since it is the sinister Vollin himself who will perish in his own cellar.

Subsequently, Boris Karloff and Bela Lugosi turn eight films together[5]. Yet, it is only in the first two in which they will be treated equally: thereafter, it was sometimes one, sometimes the other who found himself confined to a secondary role. Worse again, it was Bela Lugosi who was the most often disadvantaged compared with Boris Karloff. The story does not say whether he retained rancor or envy regarding his partner. However, according to Karloff, this placement in the background was mainly due to the difficulties Bela Lugosi had to learn English: if his accent was appreciated, his diction always suffered from this recited aspect of texts that English took in his mouth. Let's leave Boris Karloff himself to comment of this true vocal handicap: *"Poor Bela, it was strange. He was after all, a man of talent, reserved and sensible, that had made a beautiful career in classic theatre in Europe. Unfortunately, he made a fatal error, that of not having dedicated himself enough to learning our language... He really had problems at language level and he didn't know how to recite a text."*[6]

***

---

[5] See POSTSCRIPT.
[6] Cited by R. Bojarski and K. Beals dans Boris Karloff (Veyrier edition, 1976).

Two destinies that meet but don't unite: it is not said that Boris Karloff and Bela Lugosi had become private friends. Obviously, they appreciated each other, each praising the other's talent. Indeed, their reputation, so well established, would have allowed them to flee, refusing to play in the same movies. They nevertheless accepted all common roles they were offered, but still in the wave of horror cinema that began at that time and that we'll now run through.

CHAPTER 3

Fantastic and horror cinema

In the US, the emerging cinema will generate its most promising type, one we often didn't dare represent on the scene[7] : the horror type – more easily named "terror" in that time.

***

The cinema, then silent, insisted on the face's expression and the scene-play of the comedians. It's exactly what will give its most striking aspect to the gender. The spoken cinema, according to the opinions of many fans, was able to restore an authentic atmosphere of anxiety through special effects, more contemporary of our time. In the previous chapter, I have already mentioned the extraordinary expressiveness of Bela Lugosi in *Dracula*. We may as well mention that of Max Schreck in *Nosferatu the vampire*[8].

The first names that have to be mentioned as pioneers of the horror gender in the cinema, then still at its beginning, are those of makers Tod Browning and James Whale, as well as actor and makeup artist Lon Chaney. I have already mentioned them briefly before; let us study them in more detail, for the seventh Art truly gives them this honor.

***

Tod Browning (1880-1962), even if he began his career in a circus, he was a child of the dance: he had run from his family at 18 to become a clown in this circus, by love for a horsewoman. Then, becoming an actor, he put in play his own movies, thanks to actor Lon Chaney's complicity (1183-1930), child of deaf-mute parents, well-known it all the studios, he combined the abilities of comedian and makeup artist: he

---

[7] Only once with Dracula in 1927, where Bela Lugosi appeared before going back to the cinema (see previous chapter).

[8] See next chapter.

made his own makeup, sometimes making use of strong dentures, hard to endure. They called him "the man with thousands faces", an ability which made him famous with the appearance of the cinema. It was starting with 1914 he began his collaboration with Tod Browning, to then reveal strongly prolific with over eleven films that got them together in a decade. We'll mention the two most known, somewhat lost today: *The Stranger* and *London after midnight* (1927). The premature disappearance of the comedian, due to cancer of the throat, was the only cause for the ending of this incomparable duo of pioneers. Lon Chaney's celebrity and the emotion felt by his cruel ending, was so intense, that the *Marines* made a guard of honor on the day of his funeral. The tomb in which he was buried doesn't have, strangely enough, no inscription. We can see a form of modesty that suits the genius of the person.

***

James Whale (1189-1957) is especially known for the making of two movies, the first film adaptation of Mary Shelley's novel *Frankenstein* – that would give the main *Frankenstein*, followed two years later by *The Bride of Frankenstein*. I mention further and in detail the genesis of the novel and the two films[9]. Moreover, can we say that it is the meeting of James Whale with Boris Karloff that assured the celebrity of the two films, the actor and the director, or is it the reverse? In my opinion, the two options are equally true. These two titles immediately come to mind when we mention the comedian and the filmmaker, which makes them inseparable in the memory of terror cinema fans.

Certainly, the life of James Whale seems erased because little is known, compared to that of Boris Karloff as soon as he became, thanks to these two films, this director's favorite actor. It's not surprising: as a writer only lives through his books, a maker lives through his films, becoming in a way a product of the product. Of course, applying this term to dedicated works like the ones I mentioned, could seem a sacrilege, unless we consider that the cinema of the time was a work of art, instead of the true routine consumer product of our days.

***

---

[9] See Chapter 4 and 5.

Coming back to the duo Whale-Karloff, to transform it in a triumvirate of the horror movie, by adding an essential accomplice: the makeup artist Jack Pierce (11898-1958). Here as well, we can not imagine the horror gender of the cinema without knowing what it owes to the specialist, who became famous for the mask of the monster *Frankenstein* – to such a point where we could say that Boris Karloff awes his most known "face" – or rather his most brilliant appearance on the screen. His masks, though sophisticated, seemed less painful to wear than those of Lon Chaney – I will talk about this later on[10].

A year before, Jack Pierce had made up Bela Lugosi in *Dracula*. True, I have already talked about the undeniable talent of the comedian in such an interpretation; we must, however, recognize that it is Jack Pierce who was able to highlight his straight hair, his oval face and most of all the terrifying look of the vampire count, with the addition of white around the eyes, carefully lit during filming. No one doubts that the two comedians owed their celebrity as much to their makeup artists, as well as to their producers. It is unfortunate that nowadays artists as Jack Pierce disappeared in favor of synthetic images – although they need artists of the keyboard and mouse to create them and make them move on the screen. It's especially obvious in James Cameron's *Avatar* (2009).

***

We can't not love horror cinema. We can not, however, miss everything it knew to bring to the 7th Art in general: an innate sense of drama and suspense among the directors, a consummate expression among actors and makeup artists.

Truly, cinema in general, had to go through the horror gender to acquire and deserve acclaim.

---

[10] See chapter 7.

CHAPTER 4

Frankenstein and Dracula

1 – Frankenstein

Frankenstein's character seems today less known than that of Dracula, in the sense that often, the monster with its creature are mistaken. Thus, we usefully recall that Baron Victor Frankenstein is the creator of the monster, no identity inversion between himself and his monster as the latter has no name in history.

In addition, the cinema itself may be considered largely responsible for this unfortunate confusion: indeed, in the following that James Whale gave to his *Frankenstein*, the confusion is maintained in the title of the film *The Bride of Frankenstein*. It is about giving the monster a mate and not to Baron Frankenstein, which is already engaged and will marry even, at the end of the film. The "bride" in question is but a female monster, created to annihilate the instinct of violence in the spirit of the male monster – to which its creator, a consequence of an error of his valet, had in fact unknowingly grafted an "abnormal" brain: that of a murderer. Unfortunately for the monster, his mate rejects him, even though she herself had been created with the help of human remains. A philosophy can be drawn from this failed experiment that even the masters of two bodies – two scholars unite to create the "bride" – can not be, in spite of everything, masters over the two destinies; so it is impossible for them, to the one as to the other, to consider themselves God.

Let us move our interest now to the genesis of the monster and of its creator. *Frankenstein* is first of all, a novel, born from the rich imagination of the British writer Mary Shelley, wife of the British poet Percy Shelley[11] In May 1816, they went on vacation on the shore of Lake Geneva, in a villa rented by another English

---

[11] It is true that at the time she wrote the novel, Mary was still only the Shelley mistress, but they presented themselves as a couple while Shelley was already married.

poet: Lord Byron. The incessant rain prompted them to indoor activities and discussions, that quickly turned to the evocation of Erasmus Darwin's naturalist theories – grandfather of Charles Darwin – who, in the previous century, had claimed to be able to bring the dead back to life due to galvanism. The taste of this small cenacle of writers for the fantastic gothic then prompted Byron to propose his companions to each write his own fantastic story. Only Mary Shelley finalized this project, developing, with the encouragement of Percy Shelley, what was in the beginning only a part of a novel called *Frankenstein or the modern Prometheus*. Published in 1818, its success was immediate, despite the unflattering image of the Gothic gender, considered from its birth of bad taste in the literary field. This bad reputation disappeared of itself in front of the popularity to the public, which will transmit much later from literature to the cinema.

So, the monster of Frankenstein was the star role of Boris Karloff, the one that brought him glory and fame. The recipe for success had been exploited in the American style, in the sense that it first knew a third and following of the living star actor: *The Son of Frankenstein*, shot by Rowland V. Lee in 1939. This pursuit of the romantic plot was an opportunity to bring Boris Karloff in the role of the monster and Bela Lugosi in the role of Ygor, a deformed shepherd reveals to Dr. Frankenstein – son of the baron Frankenstein – that the monster is still alive, hidden in a crypt and plunged into an artificial coma. Yielding to the naive desire to rehabilitate the memory of his father, young Frankenstein awakens the monster – still by electric impulses, the method having worked before! – but he will be betrayed by Ygor, who uses the monster to take revenge on the jurors who had sentenced him to death. Following incredible chases, everything ends well for the young Frankenstein who permanently eliminates the monster by throwing it into a well of boiling sulfide.

When *The Bride of Frankenstein* got out, Boris Karloff received a lot of letters from children who pitied the fate of the monster: at that time, the unfortunate creature aroused great compassion, notably with the young public, as well as with everyone – and even as another monster: his "bride"! – rejected him. Still, it wasn't the same when *The son of Frankenstein* appeared, without doubt, because in this third version, the monster was presented not as a victim, but as a great executioner. Note that it still remains a victim because is it to serve his evil designs that deadly Ygor convinces the heir of Baron Frankenstein to revive the monster.

It was undoubtedly from this third component that Mel Brooks took his inspiration from in 1974, in his *Frankenstein junior*. The burlesque version he made is well-known. However, it raises the same philosophical inquiry as previous versions: the monster (Peter Boyle), brought back to life by an heir of Baron Victor Frankenstein (Gene Wilder), is still a victim since he ends up revolting against its maker, who still wanted, to be able to revive his ancestor, making it a subject of pseudoscientific study. Nevertheless, this film uses brilliantly the burlesque trend to achieve justice for the monster: by an exchange of personalities, it acquires knowledge and reason while his "resuscitator" completely loses them. It is therefore to upset the happy ending of this story, not just saving the creator and punishing the creature, but allowing it to know, itself, a happy ending: the monster will thus prolong a bourgeois and peaceful existence, while its creator will end up among the madmen. Justice is finally done through the magic of parody!

Creator and creature then knew other interpreters in a version signed by Francis Ford Coppola in 1995. The story is treated here in a classical but complete way this time: it's its only merit, since it was enough for the maker to find new actors to create, still, the most faithful cinema version of Mary Shelley's novel. We equally signal in this movie, the performance of Robert de Niro in the role of the monster and that of Kenneth Branagh in that of Baron Frankenstein.

Finally, note that the role of the monster was taken over by Bela Lugosi in 1942 in a parody titled: *Frankenstein against the wolf man*. The vein wasn't exhausted yet! But it is especially the movie after this one that is most known: *Frankenstein's house*, made in 1944 by Erle C. Kenton. The maker boasted of having gathered in both versions the monster, Baron Frankenstein, Dracula and the Wolf Man. Indeed, these characters fight against each other before being destroyed by the providential intervention of perfectly human heroes. Last participation of Boris Karloff in the series, this didn't suit him, the role of the monster, interpreted this time by Glenn Strange. Karloff saw himself being given the role of the brother of an ex-assistant of Baron Frankenstein. That was probably what contributed to mixed reviews of this film by critics: praised by some, roundly condemned by others, including Jean Boullet which qualifies this new monster a "pale scarecrow"[12] . Michel Caen[13] didn't miss the opportunity to underline that, in a scene, Boris Karloff withdrawing a stake from the body of the vampire – played by John Carradine – which gave him a "sadistic" image of executioner, as he had already interpreted in *The Tower of London*[14].

Still, these two movies will allow the two actors to engage in a kind of crossover that had to have entertained significantly!

2 – Dracula

Dracula is a name that always makes you shudder, since it is always associated with that of the king of vampires.

Let's remember in a few words who was this famous Count Dracula. It should be noted firstly that this name is the strain of a Transylvanian noble surname: that of Count Vlad III, prince of Wallachia, who lived in the 15th century. His family had originally been called "dracul", which means "dragon" in Vlach, because they were a member of the Order of the Dragon, chivalrous body created in 1408 by Sigismund of Luxembourg. Count Vlad III was later name Vlad "Tepes", which means "Vlad the Impaler", because of the zeal he showed firstly in the fight against Mohammedan infidels, not hesitating to learn from their torture methods. He used the same against his personal enemies, thus making a reputation of sadistic cruelty in the area where he lived: near Bistra and Borgo pass.

It should also be noted that *dracul* signifies both "dragon" and "devil" in Vlach. This semantic ambiguity has been exploited in the novel *Dracula* by Bram Stoker, to emphasize the demonic aspect of his character. In 1896, the date of the first publication of the novel, gothic literature, born precisely in the 19th century, was greatly appreciated and was looking for the incarnation of the devil in all its characters. We

---

[12] In Bizarre, n°24/25, 1962.
[13] In Midi-Minuit fantastique, n°13, 1965.
[14] See chapter 6.

can also underline, like Bob Curran does, Celtic History and Folklore professor at the University of Ulster, the influence of the Irish folklore in the Dracula character, due to the kinship of Dracula and Droch Ola, expression meaning "bad blood" in Gaelic. Indeed, we do not insist on this subject since it is only a guess, as Bram Stoker never cared to reveal the sources of his inspiration.

How did Dracula become a vampire? Bram Stoker doesn't tell us. It's the reason why the producers will pass this episode under silence, with the exception of Coppola and Wes Craven[15] : with the first one, Count Vlad Dracul revolts against God after the death of his beloved wife and then devotes himself to eternal devil worship and blood; with the second one, Dracula is a reincarnation of Judas Iscariot, traitor among the apostles, and the one who handed Jesus Christ over. He has an allergy to silver caused by the 30 denier he received as the price for his treachery, and a fear of the sun evoked by a suicide at dawn.

Bela Lugosi only played once the role of Count Dracula, in 1931, in Tod Browning's movie *Dracula* – but it was the culmination of his career, as the role of the Frankenstein monster was for Boris Karloff. Otherwise, he played the main role in another movie by Tod Browning: the *Mark of the Vampire*, made in 1935, which didn't have a Count Dracula, but this time, a Count Mora: the latter, accompanied by his daughter Luna, wandered the night in the countryside draining the owls he met of their blood. This new adaptation of the myth of vampire, it seeks to furthermore stand out from the classic Dracula, pulls its originality by presenting itself as a police investigation, led by detective Neumann, more like a form of possession of the human characters by the vampire – which obviously doesn't prevent Bela Lugosi to be comfortable, playing a vampire character with the same talent as in *Dracula.*

So, Friedrich Murnay, Max Schreck, Tod Browning and Bela Lugosi, starting with 1929, were at the origin of the vampire cinema. We will now see how this gender knew to develop and impose itself.

---

[15] In Dracula 2000.

CHAPTER 5

The wave of vampire cinema

The vampire cinema owed its debut in 1922, not exactly to Count Dracula, but to the more vague term of "Nosferatu".

Within the most cultivated public, we notice, however, a slight confusion between the terms "Dracula" and "Nosferatu". The second is a Hungarian word which means "non-dead": therefore, it is also similar to a vampire, supernatural being that ensures its survival after death by feeding on the blood of humans, subsequently transforming themselves into vampires. Still, originally, even if there are others in literature and film, Nosferatu was not the second name of Dracula, since it is not presented thus in the first film version of this myth: that of Friederich Murnau, made in 1922, silent movie, highlighting the big expression qualities of actor Max Schreck in the role of a vampire who then carried the name of Count Orlok[16]. It will be reborn fifty years later – was it to celebrate this anniversary? – in *Nosferatu, ghost of the night* of Werner Herzog, putting as star actor, the German Klaus Kinski. In this movie, the confusion is really made between Nosferatu and Count Dracula, since it's effectively this character that Kinski plays.

Count Dracula is a character with multiple faces. The deformed humanoid has large, clawed hands in Murnau's film and will quickly abandon its place to the cinema and in the collective imagination, this flattering representation of an aristocrat in the prime of his life, tall and slender, with fine features, pale complexion and black hair. His dark suit and big black cape with a red lining will accentuate his fame. In reality, we find Dracula as Bram Stoker had described him only in one movie: an old man with white hair, with a wan complexion, but also able to rejuvenate himself from his victims when they satisfy him. The only horrifying detail will remain in his sharp and excessively developed canines, often dripping with blood.

---

[16] Bram Socker's widow will attack Murnau in court, reproaching of having used a similar script to his novel without first buying the rights – like in all the movies "Nosferatu: see list at the end of the chapter.

Obviously, all vampire movies will insist on the fact that he has no shadow and can't reflect in a mirror – since he's a living dead! He can transform in a bat, in a wolf, has at his disposal a superhuman power, but can be destroyed by the light of day, wholly water or a stake planted in his heart during his inactivity moments: the day, for he remains an absolute creature of the night. He can rest during the day only on the earth where he had been buried, thus obliging him to take it with him in a coffin when he moved to London with Browning and Coppola, in Amsterdam with Herzog. He can only go into a house with the complicity of one of its residents, a fact which is particularly shown in *Dracula, prince of darkness* (1959): his victim, Diana, lets Dracula in herself, in the monastery where she and her husband had taken refuge – she is also under a hypnotic influence by the Earl's will. The religious symbols, such as crucifixes and wafers, are also strong deterrent weapons against him, as the vampire myth will never divest itself of a religious aspect that makes Dracula and his minions particularly edifying symbols of the Antichrist.

Furthermore, all producers – except Murnau – will also underline his seducer character: he hypnotizes his victims and also knows how to seduce them, especially in the adaptation that Francis Ford Coppola will make in 1992. Coppola's Dracula is capable of falling in love, while Tod Browning's – as well as the one of Terence Fisher, played at the end of the '50's by Christopher Lee – only distinguishes among women his potential victims: the fascination he has over them has nothing sentimental and the possession in which he makes them fall involves nothing sexual; they are merely victims to bleed to death, like men are. The companions of the count in *Dracula's nightmare* appear as captive victims imploring the help of Jonathan Harker; Helen, murdered and transformed into a vampire by Dracula, manifests towards him submission and a morbid attachment that will stimulate the brutality of the Count in *Dracula, Prince of Darkness*. The image of the seducer remains more alive with Bela Lugosi than Christopher Lee: the cold and cruel expression on the face of the count is tempered by a white illumination that doesn't affect the vampire's eyes; the spectator can then ask himself, according to his personal sensibility, if this illumination softens or gives, on the contrary, more worrying to the face of the vampire. No doubt we should see the transcription of the physical principle of a natural inclination of the Hungarian actor who cultivated during his early years, his dandy appearance – not to say that of a playboy!

34

On the contrary, Count Dracula, interpreted by Kinski is an authentic monster: his living-dead appearance is terribly rendered by this skinny old man, the face of a white chalk, hardly human. However, this monstrous appearance doesn't prevent both Nosferatus to succumb to the charms of Mina, the bride of their visitor, Jonathan Harker: Count Orlok will scream – silently! – "Oh! What a lovely neck!" while detailing with lust, Mina's portrait; the neck is thus shown as an erogenous zone more than as the place where blood absorption is easiest! As for Dracula, played by Kinski, he will have to pass a night with Mina to finally be destroyed by the light of day: this is the only definite way in Herzog's film to defeat the vampire; so this is, again, a barely concealed evocation of the sexual act. This one, on the contrary, is more evident than in John Badham's *Dracula* (1979), in which Frank Langella plays a vampire under the appearance of a young man with an irresistible charm, the most sensual there is: after having entered Lucy Seward's room, he examines his quite willing victim, as she reveals her charms, generously unhooking her nightgown...

Tod Browning's *Dracula* addressed the concerns of the 30s about the growing emigration – overwhelming, in the public opinion – that the United States then experienced: Dracula's character thus embodied the fear of foreigners. The following, as we have seen, put forward the possession of victims and the sensual aspect of the count. Then, the vampire movie parodies, made by Roman Polanski (the *Vampire ball – 1967)* and by Mel Brooks *(Dracula dead and loving it – 1994)* insisted more on the purely burlesque side, not hesitating to turn into ridicule their vampires and victims. With Mel Brooks, Dracula will not succeed in perfectly attracting Mina, since she will stumble over many objects in her room, then mistake the door: "Mina, you're in the closet: quickly get out!" the vampire will protest! With Polanski, the son of Count Krolock, without hiding his homosexuality, tried to seduce, then bite the young Adonis, played by Polanski himself. In the middle of the other more grotesque characters, some more than others, beginning with Professor Ambrosius, who stalks him, only Count Krolock, with his cold and cynical attitude will confine to an apparent dramatic role – which only accentuates the ridicule of his entourage, humans or vampires. That is why he allows himself the joke about "sleepwalking bats" to illustrate Ambrosius' "theories", as well as the strange order: *"Sharpen your incisors!"*, launched at the vampires when in the middle of the ball, they finally realize that only two of them can be humans, being the only ones to be reflected in a large mirror! To sharpen the incisors? Wouldn't it be rather the canines, favorite weapons of the vampire? Did Polanski want to add here a burlesque note or mystify his audience? The question remains…

***

Thus, vampire movies will make a nice place in which the 7th art will grow, from its birth. There are about 650 vampire movies around the world. The two tables below cite the most representative of the genre:

1) "NOSFERATU" MOVIES

(It only "officially" represents the theme of the vampire, since the producers hadn't bought the right to Bram Stocker's novel)

Year	Title	Producer	Principal actor
1922	*Nosferatu, the vampire*	Friedrich Murnau	Max Schreck
1979	*Nosferatu, ghost of the night*	Werner Herzog	Klaus Kinski
1988	*Nosferatu in Venice*		Klaus Kinski
2000	*The shadow of the vampire*	E. Elias Merhige	Willem Dafoe

2) "DRACULA" MOVIES

(They constitute a true and official adaptation of Bram Stocker's novel)

Year	Title	Producer	Principal actor
1931	*Dracula*	Tod Browning	Bela Lugosi
1958	*The nightmare of Dracula*	Terence Fischer	Christopher Lee
1959	*Dracula, prince of darkness*	Terence Fischer	Christopher Lee
1973	*Dracula and his vampire women*	Dan Curtis	Jack Palance
1979	*Dracula*	John Badham	Frank Langella
1992	*Dracula*	Francis Ford Coppola	Gary Oldman
2012	*Dracula*	Dario Argento	Thomas Kretschmann

CHAPTER 6

Continuation of careers

Boris Karloff and Bela Lugosi after 1931

Like I have said before[17], Boris Karloff and Bela Lugosi form a quasi-inseparable tandem for some years, not by their will, but following the eminently advertising desire of their employer: Carl Lammle, of PDG Universal.

The main idea – which was to ensure the revenue – imposed by itself: the two actors who had triumphed in two horror movies of great success: *Frankenstein* and *Dracula,* had to be united for other horror movies, for which their common playing would assure a success, supposedly phenomenal. In reality, if the six movies they made together had a global success, they never equaled the previous two, remaining a continuance of their careers of which both actors, could have surely, done without.

I will not give details about these eight movies, of so little importance, truth be told. I have already detailed *The Black Cat* and *The Raven*[18]. I will content myself by presenting here the most representative, considered today as the developers for the horror cinema of the 30s and 40s.

Before that, I would like to quote a short movie, similar to a screen test – without wanting to insult two so experienced actors! – that Boris Karloff and Bela Lugosi had to play, placing them face to face in a very brief secret meeting in which they seem to distrust each other:

'You live with the dead, Bela', Karloff said, deadpan. 'Whoever wins the game will lead the Grand Parade of the studios!'

'OK, Boris!' Lugosi replied, falsely phlegmatic.

And they both burst out laughing.

This film piece ensured the presentation of *The Black Cat* and was part of an advertising trailer. Moreover, we must note that these words quite enigmatic, perhaps unwittingly evoked the future

---

[17] See chapter 2.
[18] See chapter 2.

forced collaboration of Karloff-Lugosi. Indeed, they were made to play sinister stories, all based on fear, of course, and who conjured particular pronounced mortuary situations.

Let's also mention Lambert Hillyer's *The invisible ray* (1936), where Boris Karloff played a character which will be familiar to him because it was: of a scholar that a nice discovery transforms into a destructive madman. The film was to have a sequel – a series of sequels even, that are still struggling in our days to exploit the "vein", which will became a hit movie. Still, the public's disinterest then for the movie within the imaginary condemned this project. It will only be resumed in 1940, with Lionel April and Lon Chaney Junior instead of Karloff and Lugosi. One of those ironies that only knows to spare the genius of cinema, nevertheless profited Bela Lugosi, that turned *The Phantom Creeps*, a drama using the scraps of *The invisible ray* in 1939.

Arthur Lubin's *Black Friday* (1940) shows Boris Karloff in the role of a genius surgeon, Dr. Sovac, making an unbelievable brain transplant between a university professor and a gangster, played by Stanley Ridges. The surgeon nevertheless proceeds, with a mercantile aim, hypnotizing his patient so he would find his gangster personality, thus leading him to the hidden plunder. The result is a fantastic series of changes in personalities, in truth, difficult to follow. It must be noted however, that Bela Lugosi is not treated according to his merits in this film, whose stars are unquestionably Karloff and Ridges. He only has a minor role that they will try in vain to shine with some artifices, including the scene of his death. Yet it was Lugosi which had to, originally, play the dual role of teacher-gangster! Why this injustice? No wonder it brought the demise of movies bringing together the famous tandem of terror at Universal.

It's actually at RKO that Boris Karloff and Bela Lugosi played their last movie together: *Body Snatchers* by Robert Wise (1945). Strange fact, they were the main starts on the poster, while the starring role was played by Henry Daniell; they needed to take care once again of the demands of advertising. Again, however, the scenario reserved for Bela Lugosi a minor role as a servant. Should we see the beginning of his downfall? It's what we'll see later on.

***

Boris Karloff's cinema career was more thriving than that of Bela Lugosi. It is an undeniable fact that has its source after 1931, making him a popular actor, compared to his Hungarian counterpart. Let's say it frankly: Bela Lugosi, even if officially he was an American citizen starting with 1927, won't ever truly be one in the public's spirit... and maybe in that of the producers' as well: when we know, for example, that many years later, they'll make Bruce Lee mask himself in black in order to not steal the light from Van Williams in *The green hornet*, we immediately understand the xenophobia from which American cinema will suffer for a long time, and which was, without doubt, at the origin of Bela Lugosi's decline.

During this time, Boris Karloff continued on a roll not really unprecedented but that had to reveal his immense talent.

His greatest success, following *Frankenstein*, was decidedly Karl Freund's *The Mummy* (1932). This film was to mark the imagination to the point that a remake was dedicated to it many years later[19]. The awakening of the high priest of ancient Egypt, Imhotep, reincarnated as Hadrath Bey after his exhumation by Egyptologists of the 20th century, can be interpreted as a sort of revenge against those who, in his time, had thwarted his love deemed "guilty" with an Egyptian princess, whom he wanted to resurrect after stealing a papyrus containing a magic formula. This is what tends to make the outset of the character Hadrath Bey friendly, if he didn't however, become immoral to want to steal the soul of his beloved, because it was reincarnated in the person of the young pretty Helen Grosvenor, fiancée of another Egyptologist. The threats and constraints in front of which he will not recede, in order to satisfy his personal desires, will kill the sympathy the viewer had felt until then for Imhotep. It's precisely this duality between two characters, the first being reincarnated in the second, that makes this movie infinitely subtle and will ensure its success, much more than the fantastic appearance and vaguely horrifying plot – vaguely, yes, for the scene of the awakening of the mummy is only suggested in a roundabout way: the horrified expression and the screams of the young Egyptologist, who unintentionally caused its return to life; we barely get to see the shadow of the mummy releasing his bandages

---

[19] Stephen Sommer's The Mummy (1999).

and getting out of his sarcophagus! Of course, the cinema of that time would have caused blackouts in the rooms, protests in any case, probably even an outright ban, pure and simple, if it had exhibited all the details of this scene of horror – to the great disappointment of the spectators of our time!

Obviously, his greatest successes, as his grandest appearances on the big screen were made under the mask of the monster Frankenstein. Thus, two titles need to be remembered: *The bride of Frankenstein* (1935) and *The son of Frankenstein* (1940). Although very marked by this character in the public eye, Boris Karloff won't play the role of monster in Howard Koch's *Frankenstein 1970* in 1958, but that of the creator, Doctor Victor Frankenstein. Did they finally want to separate the creature from its creator, to better respect Mary Shelley's novel? Let's rather say that this "remake" – which wasn't one – wanted at the same time to follow the new wave of horror movies and modernize the myth: Doctor Frankenstein is believed to have survived the torture of the Nazis during World War II, which explains the makeup seamed with scars that Boris Karloff had to wear. Besides, the monster itself, played by Mike Lane, he didn't show his face, but rather resembles a giant mummy, covered in bandages as it is. The maker, equally insists, always following the trend of the time, on the dangers of nuclear power, since it is atomic energy, manipulated by its creator, who gives life back to the monster, before radiations end up killing them both.

We must also retain the composition of other roles that marked the career of Boris Karloff. Since 1932, so, just after *Frankenstein*, he played in Charles Brabin's *The mask of Fu Manchu*, the cruel character of Fu Manchu, Asian potentate, who after a series of adventures, dreams of having the golden mask and sword of Gengis Khan, with the goal to unite the Asian people in the conquest of the world. History was about to illustrate this cinematographic theme, from the novel by Sax Rohmer, since Japan had decided, from that year forth to forcibly open new markets by launching first of all to conquer the Chang Kai-shek's[20] China. Other "Chinese" roles were given to Boris Karloff in the character of the Sinoamerican detective James Lee Wong (1938

---

[20] Modern Spelling: Jiang Jieshi.

40

and 1939). Indeed, the time was not for the glorification of actors of Asian descent! I wrote earlier that Bruce Lee, was not allowed to steal Van William's star light in movie *The Green Hornet*; similarly, although he was at the origin of the script, they will refuse him the right to interpret the role of Kwai Chang Caine in the *Kung Fu* series, preferring David Carradine. This happened in the 60s and 70s, which had thus inherited the xenophobic spirit of the 30s, since they would rather use Westerners to interpret fake Chinese, after having curbed their eyes, dyed their skin with makeup and transformed their faces with wigs!

I have already underlined the extraordinary adaptation of Boris Karloff's expressions, under all disguises. We could almost see in him a disciple of Lon Chaney, since the actor knew how to make all faces in a natural way. Le Petit Larousse and Petit Robert 2, in the time when they still cited Karloff – they're not doing it anymore! – were not mistaken, since it is under the guise of the executioner Mord they once exhibited pictures of the actor. The film *The London Tower* by Rowland V. Lee (1939) presents Karloff in one of most sinister roles, not hesitating to present him with a shaved head and a huge ax, then carefully show him honing his knives in his torture room. Such representations rather lend a smile in our time, when horror films significantly stress other infinitely more bloody and sadistic cruelty! We will rather remember the talent of the actor, whose belief in the role and professionalism are well established.

Towards the end of his career, Boris Karloff will give his best again in the *Unconquered*, by the legendary producer Cecil B. de Mille (1947). Nonetheless, we will regret the injustice made to Boris Karloff, who will not interpret the Indian chief Guyasota, the star's role being held by Gary Copper, assisted by his partner Paulette Goddard. Did the star of the "monster" not like the British actor anymore? Still, I remember being very impressed, when I was a teenager and saw this movie for the first time. I strongly remember my indignation noticing that Boris Karloff wasn't playing the star role, for I had seen almost all adaptations of the monster Frankenstein. How could the actor be used like that? He still seemed very impressive in a scene, the ruthless Indian chief, he proclaimed before a settler of the white community: *"When torch has burned all killed!"* prompting the bewilderment of adults and cries of terror from children. Oh no, he was not done scaring, the terrible Boris Karloff!

This was exactly the fate of Bela Lugosi. After his masterful interpretation of Dracula, we can say he wasn't able to survive this role: vampire by day, vampire always! He had to constantly supply terror to the viewer in this role that the enthusiasm of producers and of the public had made him wear! It's the only reason for which Bela Lugosi was condemned to horror films, just like Boris Karloff: particularly evidenced in these two works from 1932 which assured him the star role: *Chandu, the Magician* by William-Cameron Menzies and Marcel Varnel and *Doctor Moreau's Island* by Erle C. Kenton. In the first one, he plays Roxor, a mad scientist who searches to invent a death ray to conquer the world; in the second, wearing a bestial and hairy face, he plays the "guardian of the lay", while Charles Laughton holds the star role: that of Doctor Moreau. After the movie series he'll make with his friend Boris Karloff, he played roles of monsters and vampires, especially in *Mark of the vampire*[21], then in *Wolf Man*, where his character is named Bela! I have already said that this last film will make the object of a parody in 1942: *Frankenstein meets the wolf man*, where he'll wear a mask of the monster, giving the line to Lon Chaney Junior! Incredible! There are crosses, coincidences whose taste remain bitter... !

Moreover, Bela Lugosi had to endure tough disappointments during and mostly after the World War II. During the war, he displayed great generosity by creating a committee of Hungarian anti-fascist in the US, to come to the help of European victims of Nazism. During this time, he could return to the theater in the play *Arsenic and old lace* by Joseph Kesselring, where he played the role interpreted in the past with great success by Boris Karloff! Sad turn of events, he wasn't accepted – not more than Boris Karloff actually! – to replay the role in a cinema version of the play, made by Frank Capra: they preferred Raymond Massey. Worst yet, he had to give his place to John Carradine for the vampire role in *The Home of Dracula* and *The Home of Frankenstein*. He will not find the vampire theme again until 1944 in *The return of the vampire* by Lew Landers – but there as well, even if he was again decked in his famous black cloak, he did not

---

[21] Op. cit. previous chapter.

play the role of Count Dracula. There are improbabilities likely to question the credibility of writers and directors!

After that, Bela Lugosi had to adapt to compromises that hurt his self-esteem and credibility of fantastic cinema. The type – without doubt because we find it truly inferior to the atrocities revealed by the World War II – were strongly declining in the public's spirit. Even if he made horror movies, their sloppy intrigues couldn't allow him performances like the one that made him famous in his first screen appearances. His only color film: *Scared to death* by Christy Cabanne (1947) showed him thin and weakened by disease – he was already 65 years old! It was probably not only for the needs of the script that he played sporting a fake beard, a soft hat and glasses! Then, ensuring only the utilities in third level works, and only to gain a living, Bela Lugosi didn't have any other engagement to the screen until 1955. During this time, his wife, Lilian had divorced him, taking with her their son, Bela Junior, heartbreaking for the old actor that was already worn by disease, and whose bank account was dangerously close to red...

Bela Lugosi, must therefore comply with many requirements, due to the cinema as well as on a daily basis to a career he loved passionately. Boris Karloff, who shared the same passion, was forced from the moment where fame took him in her claws, often more painful that soothing. This is what I invite you to visit with me now.

CHAPTER 7

Talent: a need to adapt

If Boris Karloff and Bela Lugosi had imagined themselves, at the beginning of their careers, that only talent was enough to ensure fame and even credibility to the actor, they were strongly mistaken. Indeed, before the success of the actor is the success of the film itself, a commercial product by excellence that made the actor a product of the product, like I have already underlined[22].

Lon Chaney had understood it first, Boris Karloff had to compel later: a star role in a horror movie, ensuring thus by makeup and its accessories, by the personal's contribution of the actor. This is notably the case of a part which requires wearing a mask and all kinds of wigs, such as that of the Frankenstein monster.

Let's give this justice to the actor: his head and his face carved with an ax served the mask more than the monster mask served its character. We'll see it later with Bela Lugosi when he was made to wear a similar mask[23] : his oval face and the regular shape of his head couldn't inspire Jack Pierce as well as Boris Karloff's skull. The makeup artist did the sketches and then transformed them, corrected to make the faces of the monster as he had imagined it. So it's Boris Karloff's head that created the mask. Jack Pierce confesses it himself: he had been "fascinated" by Karloff's face. It is fitting that, subsequently, the face became in the eyes of the general public the same symbol of Frankenstein, to the point of definitely reaching a confusion between the creator and the creature?

It was later that the mask took its revenge, if we can say this: Boris Karloff had to wear it with every public appearance to each forced commitment. To don the mask, he was made to pass three hours in the makeup studio – which forced him to be from sunrise

---

[22] See previous chapter 5.
[23] In Frankenstein meets the werewolf by Roy William Neill (1943).

to dawn on the set. In addition, the mask was painful to wear: each fitting was torture for Boris Karloff who had never endured this kind of pain and he thought it often to be insurmountable! Trials he still suffered without protest – see how far passion for movies leads!

It was still worse when shooting: I have already said it, Boris Karloff naturally had a powerful frame, but it was probably not considered sufficiently "monstrous"! He was obliged to wear a thick padding under his suit, which increased his form and helped him give that stiff gait that characterizes the monster. Bad luck for the actor, filming took place in summer, which exhausted him because his body was quickly flooded with sweat; in addition, after each needed break, he had to put on his soaked disguise again, full of sweat, not having time to dry. Poor Boris who sweated very much, to offer us this unforgettable experience! He, however, laughed reviewing his character evolve, admitting with a smile, during the whole shooting, he had the impression of *"being in a shroud, which no doubt contributed to strengthening the realism!"*

Another advantage of the actor in this silent but eloquent role: his eyes. According to Jack Pierce and James Whale: *"they reflected all the sufferings of the unfortunate creature bereft of speech, contrasting with his hideous appearance and fearful strength."* The public wasn't mistaken, since the monster aroused its compassion!

Anyway, we can mention the courage of the actor, not only in wearing the complete disguise, but also in certain key scenes – especially in those where the monster, not yet loved, is surrounded by lightning and thunder. Imagine poor Boris Karloff lying half naked on the operating table, while above it, technicians were handling the blades for white-hot lightning to appear! He prayed that their skill in handling such instruments knew no failure! What an actor, what impresario would be willing to take such risks without incurring the wrath of his insurance company!

Boris Karloff wasn't finished with the binding disguises. Actually, it was worst, according to him, when he made *The Mummy*. Jack Pierce, at the peak of his art, imposed him to wear not only half rotten strips, but also cotton balls and a special paint to give him the appearance of a mummy, an old Egyptian from centuries later. A veritable torture for Imhotep-Karloff! One can legitimately think that when Imhotep morphed into Hadrath Bey,

46

he suffered less than with his makeup for the mummified priest: it's then that Boris Karloff's talent affirms again, to show us this impressive character, with a sinister look, conquering stature and a resounding voice, that makes him the relentless architect of a terrible desire for justice... !

***

We have to admit: in appearance, Bela Lugosi didn't suffer the torments of his friend Boris Karloff – or, at least, not the same.

His biggest disappointment might be having shot fewer films that Karloff: 150 against more than sixty over that – some, of course, having been lost. Nonetheless, it is true that Bela Lugosi showed himself to be more hesitant, and at the same time, more demanding than Boris Karloff in the choice of his roles – at least, what he could choose. The eclecticism which might be suggested by Boris Karloff's career, given the extreme diversity of roles that he interpreted, is indeed apparent: he knew immediately what characters would suit him, without confining himself to specific roles. On the contrary, Bela Lugosi, tended to be locked in his own image, in fact, to that of Dracula in which he is still worldwide known today. His hesitant temperament often inspired him less valuable choices. According to his own confession, he: *"never knew how to make good choices, those that Boris felt by instinct."* Karloff himself added: *"I managed to live well, Bela less."*

Moreover, Bela Lugosi's sympathies for communism, at least for the freedom that this ideology seemed to promise the artists are well known. I already quoted those he put into practice during his early days in his country[24]. The taste for mutual aid associations to the leftist trend had remained: we have already seen the one he made during the war against the regime of Admiral Horthy in Hungary[25]. After the conflict, Bela Lugosi followed trade union activities that brought upon him the suspicions of the authorities. The time was the beginning of the Cold War between the United States and the Soviet Union and, consequently, extreme mistrust of communism Americans conservatives. McCarthyism is the main

---

[24] See chapter 1.
[25] See chapter 6.

illustration: this ideology, the work of Senator Joseph McCarthy, began to index anyone proved or suspected of sympathies for the communists. Bela Lugosi was a victim, and even if he never had to do with justice, he lived his career suffering at least as far as the public's disinterest in horror films[26].

The aging actor was not consoled to see himself be moved away from the fantastic, and Providence must have heard him in 1944, as it is this year he turned his *Return of the vampire* by Lew Landers. Disappointment: he wasn't given the role of the vampire, who went to Matt Willis. Still, the secondary character he interpreted, resembled almost trait by trait Dracula: he is Bela Lugosi or he isn't! This is what led Universal to demand rights from Columbia, the film's producer for illegal loan – claim that remained unheeded.

***

I have already mentioned the differences in mentality existing between our two favorite actors. We have to admit that, first of all, they obviously correspond to the two characters, diametrically opposed: the habits of English gentleman of Boris Karloff, following the strict education he had received, contrasting notably with a more bohemian character, and at the same time, more worldly than Bela Lugosi. Moreover, Boris Karloff naturally left his characters as soon as he left the set, which Bela Lugosi had a hard time doing, it seems... Truth or legend? Let's try to answer in the next chapter.

---

[26] At least for the classic horror film: the audience wanted more inventiveness, Hollywood screenwriters drew on memories of the War to submit to the viewers the War of the Worlds or the Thing from another world, which presented more elaborate intrigues involving humans struggling with alien monsters from space.

CHAPTER 8

Two decidedly dissimilar endings

Bela Lugosi was five years older than Boris Karloff. The first dies at 74, the second at 81. The first had to slow down his shooting sessions and especially give up all travel, the second obstinately refused, going to Mexico to shoot in a wheelchair, a series that he did not finish. Such is the summary of their two ends. So I'm going to give a brief description.

***

Boris Karloff gave, until his last breath this appearance of unwavering strength he had always presented in life and on screen. When he turned to television in his later years, his health declined sharply due to heart failure who had pursued him all his life, but he still refused to retire, ignoring his doctor's advice.

I especially remember an episode from *The Wild Wild West*, where he played, in company of Robert Conrad and of Ross Martin, the role of an eccentric maharajah[27]. I didn't recognize him. It's true he had always known how to adapt to all his characters, to feel alright with all disguises. As a teenager, I had discovered this episode and what a surprise I had, to see him mentioned in the generic in the role of Rajah Singh! *"What! I thought. A great international star like Boris Karloff accepts to shoot in such an unpopular series like that?"* I could almost pity him, young film enthusiast that I was at 14 and already knowing then almost all the old movies dedicated to the myth of Frankenstein. True, I am and always have been a fan of *The Wild Wild West*, but I thought that a star like the creator of the Frankenstein monster, could take such a low value role. I tried to imagine the investment to which the producers of the series had had to consent to in order to settle the hiring of such a famous star!

---

[27] The Wild Wild West – "The night of the golden cobra" (1967).

Later, I discovered that I was wrong with everything: Boris Karloff played that character because, according to his sixth sense, he felt well in his skin. As an actor, he gave himself to art by love of art, so he played for the pleasure of playing rather than money. Such actors must really be rare nowadays!

It's during the year following the death of Bela Lugosi he played the son of Doctor Frankenstein in *Frankenstein 70*, a movie somewhat resembling a parody, which exploits the new wave of horror movies, in which they will not hesitate to put a new face to classical successful films. When he was asked if he didn't regret being assimilated to the role of monster, that followed him all his life and beyond, Karloff answered: *"I was lucky: when the producers bet on a star, they have to spend a fortune to impose a brand image, they gave it to me for free. (...) I am convinced that I would have been truly good in the role of little Lord Fauntleroy, but who would have given a cent to see that?"*

Always ready to sacrifice himself to the demon of comedy, Boris Karloff didn't hesitate to leave for Mexico to shoot a series of TV movies. Still, his health was more than threatened: additionally to an arthritis that got to a critical stage and required him to move with braces, he contracted pneumonia in England and another in Spain. The extreme pulmonary fatigue that resulted compelled the use on the Mexican film set of an oxygen tank to alleviate the damaging effects of altitude in Mexico City. Painfully, Karloff ended the series, but a new travel in the country of his ancestors was fatal: he died, exhausted by his respiratory illness, February 2, 1969.

***

Did Bela Lugosi show himself more reasonable than his friend at the end of his life – medically, at least? We can doubt it, even if he accepted to let himself be treated during his frequent hospitalizations due to unbearable pain. Unfortunately, the taste for comedy, that he had, at least as much as his friend Boris, was the reason for the appearance of this wisdom, since he quickly began taking "pills" that in reality contained morphine overdose: so he became addicted to this drug that, like all the others, becomes dangerous when taken outside a strict medical prescription.

50

On a personal level, Bela Lugosi knew, according to a persistent legend, an end of life of the strangest.

For his fans – who frequently wrote him – and for Hollywood, Bela Lugosi remained Dracula. Worse yet: he *was* Count Dracula in person. That is why the biographers are forced to live in a big house built specifically for him and whose appearance imitated Castle Dracula in the Carpathians, as shown in the film of Tod Browning. Inside, the walls, painted black, endured the panoplies topped with spears and poisoned arrows. Black cats moved between the rooms and the service was ensured by Asian domestics, all deaf and mute! As for Bela Lugosi himself, it seems he only dressed in black. Some even say that he only went out at night, daylight wounding his eyes and he slept in a coffin, like his illustrious character!

The truth and common sense bustle slightly thin in this mixture of both melodramatic and vaguely disturbing for the mental health of the person that went through them. This house, its decorations, its inhabitants and Bela Lugosi's games, effectively make you think to a sort of permanent play, lived by the actor that didn't have, like Boris Karloff, the chance to freely being offered a brand image! Still, it's not wrong to think that Bela Lugosi's taste for costumed comedy found his account!

The last role of the actor established a connection evident and at the same time, distant with this perpetual set: *Plan 9 From Outer Space* by Edward D. Wood tells, midway through science-fiction and fantastic, the story of aliens looking to raise the dead and by making them allies to rule the Earth. Bela Lugosi was supposed to play the role of a zombie, but he could only shoot some basic scenes. On the fifth day of shooting, Bela Lugosi didn't turn up on the set: he had died of a heart attack.

The death of Bela Lugosi was one of the most ordinary, since he died in his bed, August 16, 1956, while reading the script for this role in this last movie he didn't get to finish. His second wife, who had married him the year before – he was 73! – discovered him like this, coming back from daily shopping. Just another death for the man we wanted at all costs to turn into a vampire!

The funeral itself remained in the memory of the gullible – or have they been exploited by Hollywood writers, as were those of Bruce Lee in Hong Kong in *The Game of Death*? Still, he was buried coated with Count Dracula's[28] cape and the end of this discreet burial was, they said, by the flight of a huge bat gushing his tomb before the stone was sealed! This only leaves to revive Boris Karloff as Dr. Frankenstein did for his monster for the myth to be complete!

The fact is nevertheless true that Bela Lugosi remains a legend still more alive than Boris Karloff: they went to shoot the film of his life in 1995. We're talking about *Ed Wood*, a movie in which Tim Burton also retraces the life of the director of *Plan 9 From Outer Space*[29] ; the role of Bela Lugosi is played by Martin Landau[30].

***

"Sacred monsters", literally and figuratively, Boris Karloff and Bela Lugosi are among the pioneers, not only in the cinema gender, but most of all, in cinema itself. Their equals are named Charlie Chaplin, Laurel and Hardy, W.C. Fields and the Marx Brothers – to only mention a few. Without them, cinema would have, no doubt, not known such a craze among the international public. I have already said it that cinema wouldn't have even existed without horror movies. But it, itself, wouldn't have known the attachment of the public without Boris Karloff and Bela Lugosi. This reasoning is not as easy as it looks: such interpreters have developed our imaginations just by their inherent qualities of actors. So it seems, beforehand, impossible to dispense with them, and pretend to replace them.

---

[28] Not according to his own will, but that of his wife and daughter.
[29] Modified many times, this film came out in 1959.
[30] Actor most known for his interpretations in the TV series Mission impossible and Cosmos 1999.

POSTSCRIPT

General filmography

NB : bold titles and characters are those who have particularly marked the careers of both actors.

1 – Boris Karloff :

Year	Title of movies	Character played
1919	*The Masked Rider* *His Majesty, The American*	Mexican A spy
1920	*The Last of the Mohicans*	An Indian
1921	*Without Benefit Of Clergy*	Ahmed Khan
1922	*The Man From Downing Street* *Omar The Tentmaker*	Maharadjah Jehan Imam Mowaffak
1923	*The Prisoner*	Prince Kapolski
1924	*Dynamite Man*	Tony Garcia
1925	*Parisian Nights* *The human frontier*	Pierre Bit Part
1926	*The Eagle of the Sea*	A pirate
1927	*Tarzan And The Golden Lion*	Owaza
1928	*The Little Wild Girl*	Maurice Kent
1929	*The Unholy Night*	The Lawyer Abdul
1931	*Pardon Us* *The Mask of Fu Manchu* ***Frankenstein***	The tiger Ned Galloway **The Monster**
1932	*Scarface* *The Mask of Fu Manchu* *The Mummy*	Gaffney Dr. Fu Manchu Imhotep (Ardath Bey)
1933	*The Ghoul* *The House of Rothschild*	Pr. Morlant Comte Ledrantz
1934	*The Black Cat*	Hjalmar Poelzig
1935	*The Raven* *Bride of Frankenstein*	Bateman **The Monster**
1936	*The Walking Dead Juggernaut* *The Man Who Changed His Mind*	John Ellman Dr. Sartorius Dr. Laurience
1937	*West of Shanghai*	General Wu Yenfang
1938	*Mr. Wong, Detective*	James Lee Wong

1939	*Son of Frankenstein*	**The Monster**
	The Mystery Of Mr. Wong	James Lee Wong
	Mr. Wong In Chniatown	James Lee Wong
	Tower of London	
1940	*The Fatal Hour*	James Lee Wong
	Black Friday	Dr. Sovac
	Doomed To Die	James Lee Wong
1944	*The Climax*	Dr. Hohner
	House of Frankenstein	**Dr. Niemann**
1947	*The Secret Life of Walter Mitty*	Dr. Hollingshead
	Unconquered	Chef Guyasuta
1958	*Frankenstein – 1970*	**Baron Frankenstein**
1965	*Die, Monster, Die!*	Nahum Witley
1967	*The Sorcerers*	Pr. Monserrat
1968	*House of Evil Targets*	Matthias Morteval Byron Orlok
1954-56	*The adventures of Colonel March*	**TV series**
1962	*The Paradine Trial*	Colonel March
1966	*The Grinch who wanted to steal Christmas*	Juge Horfield
	Mysteries of the West	
1971	*The Incredible Invasion*	Le Grinch Mr. Singh
1972	*The Fear Chamber*	**Posthumous Movies**
		Pr. Mayer
		Dr. Mandel

2 – Bela Lugosi :

Year	Title of movies	Character played
1920	*Dr. Warren's crime*	The butler
	The last of the Mohicans	Chingachgook
1924	*Tears of clown*	The clown
1925	*The Midnight Girl*	Nicolas Schuyler
	Daughters Who Pay	Serge Romonsky
	The Thirteenth Chair	Inspector Delzante
1931	**Dracula**	**Dracula**
1932	**Murders in the Rue Morgue**	**Dr. Mirakle**
1933	*Dr. Moreau's Island*	The judge
1934	*The Black Cat*	Hjalmar Poelzig
1935	*The Mystery Of The Mary Celeste*	Anton Lerezten
	The Raven	Dr. Vollin
	Mark of the vampire	**Count Mora**
1936	*The Invisible Ray*	Dr. Bennet

1941	*The Wolf Man*	**Bela**
1942	*The Corpse Vanishes*	Dr. Lorenz
	Night monster	Pr. Brenner
	Frankenstein Meets the Wolf Man	The monster
1945	*Zombies On Broadway*	Dr. Renault
	The Body Snatcher	Joseph
1947	*Scared To Death*	Pr. Leonid
1956	*Bride of the Monster*	Dr. Vorlof
	The monsters revolt	Casimir
1959	*Plan 9 From Outer Space*	The zombie

3 – The 8 movie, uniting Boris Karloff and Bela Lugosi:

TITLE	PRODUCER	YEAR
The Black Cat	Edgar G. Ulmer	1934
Gift of Gab	Karl Freund	1934
The Raven	Louis Friedlander	1935
The invisible ray	Lambert Hillyer	1936
The son of Frankenstein	Rowland V. Lee	1939
Black Friday	Arthur Lubin	1940
You'll find out	David Butler	1940
The Body Snatcher	Robert Wise	1945

◆◆◆